Infinite Possibilities
A Haiku Journal

Infinite Possibilities
A Haiku Journal

Laurie Wagner Buyer

LCCN 2009930054
ISBN 978-0-86541-097-8
Copyright © 2009 Laurie Wagner Buyer All Rights Reserved.
Cover and interior design by Hancey Design, www.HanceyDesign.com

Filter Press, LLC
Palmer Lake, Colorado
888.570.2663
FilterPressBooks.com

This book may not be reproduced in whole or in part in any form or by any means, electronic or mechanical now known or hereafter invented, without written permission of the publisher.

Printed in the United States of America

Dedication

For the first women in my life—
my mother, Joan, and
my sisters, Karen and Eileen

Write in this Book

Each day for a year Laurie Wagner Buyer wrote a haiku.
You hold her collection in your hands. Yet this book is unfinished.
The open space on each page is for you to make the book your own.

Write in this Book to

- Explore the *Infinite Possibilities* of writing
- Record your own thoughts, feelings, or observations
- Experiment with a simple haiku, a complex sonnet, a few sentences, or an essay
- Reflect and measure the worth of your days
- Find new ways to chart the progress of a project
- Develop an outline for your future masterpiece

Write in this Book if

- You are despondent
  Get the blue thoughts out of your head
- You are happy
  Capture the moment to savor again and again
- You are anxious
  Reduce anxiety by writing about the problem
- You are undecided
  Clarify your options
- You are doubtful
  Open new pathways

Write in this Book because

- writing is affirming
- writing focuses the mind
- writing quiets the heart
- writing expands creativity
- writing can be freeing and therapeutic
- writing celebrates the one moment
- writing preserves our life-changing events

Laurie wrote for a year...one haiku per day.
Now, it is your turn.

Write in this Book

Preface

While the masters have said that poetry needs no introduction, I believe that the idea behind this small book does require some explanation. These haiku, written in 2001, evolved out of my desire to have a daily meditation as well as a routine writing exercise. I lived on a high country cattle ranch in Colorado, my husband at that time was dealing with the effects of ill health and aging, and I was finishing my MFA in Writing from Goddard College in Vermont.

Thus, the poems reflect the traditional haiku involvement of humans with the natural world, including seasonal shifts, weather changes, and encounters with wild animals. They also examine those things in everyday life that intrude on our intimacy with the earth: the escape and return of travel, complex people interaction, the simplicity of cooking and chores, the usual holidays, unexpected medical appointments, and the heart-opening demands of being a writer. The "him" in some of the poems refers to my husband. Also introduced are the dog, a dun colt in training, an old horse, an occasional cat, and, of course, the cow herd. At the close of each day, I wrote whatever image gripped my psyche. Notes in brackets are added to insure clarity as to place.

In an effort to reveal the true insightful and spare form of the haiku, I chose to use only the minimal punctuation of an opening capital and a closing period or question mark. Line breaks and dashes evoke the breath or pause between images. This book may be read from beginning to end as an unfolding story, or it can be picked up at random to read a poem here or there at any time of the day or night. Some may choose a certain day to see what happened then, or take on the study of a particular season currently being experienced. However this collection is used I hope it will be a meditation for brief moments of insight and delight. Welcome to the vanishing world of impossible beauty and humble acceptance. May the images I sought to capture illuminate other lives.

– *Laurie*

Winter

In open water
Mallard ducks paddle and swirl
mocking winter ice.

Dawn sun on pine poles
illuminates frost on bark
bright heartwood wakens.

Snow patterns in sage
a veil of lace on the face
of south fork ridges.

With a noisy rush
the fire finds a pitch pocket
and consumes itself.

Large sphere of orange light
engulfs the far horizon
unquenchable fire.

Cream cheese and walnuts
the sin of forbidden cake
I lick the beaters.

Pinto beans and ham
biscuits baked with buttermilk
the dun colt won't lead.

The house smells like love
fresh bread out of the oven
I beg for kisses.

Two below zero
full moon sets—the high divide
silver on pewter.

[to Denver]
Interstate traffic
keeps my eyes glued to my knees
passenger Zen time.

[home again]
Walking through the gate
we hold hands like new lovers
your gloved grip is strong.

Hay delivery
huge truck—big bales—many bucks
content cows feed.

Heavy gray snow skies
clouds collapse against high peaks
only a skif falls.

Dun horse in sagebrush
fast trip and fall—the sky reels
cold wind cartwheeling.

Open winter dust
dust dust dust dust dust dust dust
dirt dry and dusty.

   At last bright snowfall
like flour through a sifter screen
      all is light pastry.
              Ten below zero
        the poor dog hops on three legs
           I breathe in pure air.
                          Snow falling off wires
                      man and dog walk up white road
                          long line of blue hills.

[off to New Mexico]

Junkyard dogs bark hard
I jog on searching for some
   remnant of desert.

        The old woman sleeps
      curled tight around stolen food
        sun rises on buttes.

[home again]

Dark indigo pool
reflects back tall spruce forest
spires kiss the bank edge.

Wood smoke sheathes the house
cats curl in cardboard boxes
cold creeps through my soles.

Pain against my ribs
is my heart breaking again
or is it just age?

Dashing through the brush
the dog spooks the trotting colt
　　we all leap and flee.

　　　　　　[to Fort Logan National Cemetery]

　　　　　Geese circle the park
　　　as I eat my sandwich lunch
　　　　　　I think of kisses.　　　　Lichen on gray rock
　　　　　　　　　　　pale green-orange against the snow
　　　　　　　　　　　　　the long age of loss.

[to Woodland Park]

Four-point buck tongues seed
  from a frozen bird feeder
    his tail flips pleasure.

[to Burlington, Vermont]

Light chop on water
Lake Champlain is blue on blue
behind bare branches.

[at Goddard College]

Noon sun caught in ice
summer scents frozen in time
the wind changes colognes.

                                      The white noise machine
                                      hums all night—I cannot hear
                                      if the earth still breathes.

Snowflakes fall and fall
stitching lace on every tree
the land's bridal gown.

The grave of *Silence*
is hidden under new snow
stone wall supports me.

Romantic stories
revolve around the table
each one a dessert.

Hot inside dancing
bodies twisting—twirling—light
spills from open doors.

If a kiss lingers
past midnight—past two—past dawn
will it always stay?

[in Colorado Springs]

Cottontail rabbits
hop across the frozen lawn
long cold ears laid back.

[home again]

He stays at the gate
wind tugging his hat and coat
waits for my return.

Black lace of spruce boughs
full moon rises—breast of light
caught in bark cradle.

Hard snow all day long
pastures shifting brown to white
how fast earth changes.

At twenty below
full moonlight on snow shimmers
I walk on diamonds.

Stuck in my own thoughts
I ski—see nothing—the muse
dances out of sight.

Two spike bull elk trot
through snow in front of dawn sun
glowing like candles.

                                                Going into town
                                  the road runs straight and narrow
                                        how can I be lost?

Eyes tearing I read
poems for a dying mother
and watch the fire fade.

Snowshoes slap new snow
the dog follows on packed track
through sun-speckled woods.

Splitting wood at dawn
the ax sounds cold and hollow
when it hits the stump.

Hard wind-drifted snow
gives way beneath Nordic skis
I fall down laughing.

Cold and arthritic
the old gelding tries to buck
but only crow hops.

Thin longhorn cows feed
on gold grass buried by snow
along dead willows.

Unrelenting words
all day I wrestle with words
loving the wan sun.

[to Salida]

Kidney specialist
Creatinine—MRI
new language—new fears.

[home again]

Four elk jump the fence
long life is still possible
do we pray—dare dream?

[to Colorado Springs]
Stuffed in a culvert
hammers beat on top of him
nasty modern test.

[home again]

Hard-bitten west wind
bleak sun carved out of thin clouds
peers through a window.

The sound of new fire
I cook to ease gnawing fear
spicy corn chowder.

Ponderosa pine
smells sharp and sweet in the sun
live sap waits for spring.

Small bird chirps at dawn
way too early for false spring
who sings—who sings—who?

Dancing with the Grinch
the granddaughter swings her hips
the dog leaps and barks.

Light snow falling at dusk
changing the world to winter
calm arrives and stays.

Brilliant sun burns snow
Hereford cows corralled near barn
doze and chew their cuds.

Gelding mounts the mare
she kicks and moves—kicks again
still he tries once more.

Redwing blackbirds trill
high-pitched notes from willow stems
where does winter go?

[to the Rocky Mountain Book Festival]

Logjam of people
in a wide river of books
I wait on the bank.

[home again]

Whiteface leggy calves
hide behind mothers' udders
sucking with pleasure.

                                        Big black backwards calf
                              cranked and pulled from old cow's womb
                                              will he ever walk?

                    First-light fog and mist
                snow and silence deafen all
                    except my own heart.

Willow-swishing skis
coyote calls along river
I breathe hard and fast.

                Full moon's mottled face
                caught between heavy storm clouds
                landscape burns silver.

                                          Snow caught on branches
                                          I tongue cold delicious mounds
                                          swallow winter whole.

Slick branch under snow
slips my falling feet sideways
sky turns blue then white.

Brisk western night wind
sprinkles snow with pine needles
forest trail blown in.

Redwing blackbirds sing
from a budding willow bush
cats pause to listen.

Lying on the couch
in full sun warm and content
reading and sleeping.

[To Buena Vista]

Two hours at dentist
endless list of in-town chores
blizzard coming home.

Was that a blackbird
or just the squeaky gate hinge
in my husband's hands?

Take out stove ashes
Vacuum—clean—and dust again
the house stays dirty.

Twin camp robbers perch
on snow-laden aspen branch
chirp, chatter, and scold.

Hundred head of elk
block the winter road to town
I count eight spike bulls.

                                        Poor slow old pony
                              has to stop to make droppings
                                    I wait while he groans.

Newborn calf curled still
as a fallen leaf in grass
only his eyes move.

Bluebird on a wire
two robins in aspen trees
sing false spring–false spring.

Rain drips from the eaves
gray day turns slowly to night
dawn will bring more snow.

Nineteen cow elk graze
old grass on a bare meadow
while a new storm brews.

Flanked by five coyotes
the week-old calf is gutted
beller breaks the day.

Snow stuck on his neck
the colt dances toward the barn
storms always push us.

Sunshine one second
a whirling blizzard the next
I gallop for home.

Bitter bitter breeze
breath stealer—new calf killer
grant me some release.

Between hill and clouds
a small slice of open sky
rising sun bleeds gold.

Paired geese swim circles
on mirrored mica water
surrounded by ice.

Lying face to sky
the pasture breathes beneath me
sucking melting snow.

[driving to Sterling, CO]

Rolling tumbleweed
high plains wind pushing shoving
trying to birth spring.

[at Stevens Elementary]

Children sitting in
a circle ask me questions
the train whistle blows.

                                                                 Sterling before dawn
                                                         diesel engines—train whistles
                    An open journal   robins chirp and flit.
                a soft comfortable chair
                    the scent of roses.

Buds breaking open
on giant cottonwood trees
lingerie branches.

Fresh mown grass—grilled steaks
walking unfamiliar streets
I'm not a stranger.

Train grinds to a stop
whistle blows five short sharp blasts
fifty-four cars halt.

[an unexpected visit]

Miles from home his hand
in mine feels unusual
makes me love him more.

Women write sonnets
seven lines then seven lines
scratching-pen silence.

Open-face full moon
caught in cottonwood branches
hold tight—wait for me.

Rain in the long night
glistening lakes everywhere
the earth gulps and sighs.

After the blizzard
dead branches litter the ground
snow sticks on tree bark.

[going home again]

Across open plains
spring blizzard snow piled in drifts
blessed moisture saves.

Four geese upriver
fly honking into the sun
mated forever.

White wings on blue sky
a killdeer's piercing dawn cry
I wish I could soar.

Gray weathered pine board
silver frost clings to warped grain
　　sun dissolves the sheen.

　　　　　　　Mist in the canyon
　　　　　every branch is gilded white
　　　　　　I seek scattered dreams.

　　　　　　　　　　　Three geese fly upstream
　　　　　　　　　silent except for wing beats
　　　　　　　　　where's the third one's mate?

Lake ice turns over
freed water gleams brilliant blue
twin ducks wing away.

Smoke over the ridge
settles like fine fog on trees
it begins to snow.

Like a purple bruise
a huge thumbprint cloud darkens
the sky's pale dawn skin.

After the blizzard
fifty head of grazing elk
brown and buff on white.

Whispering from mist
great blue heron flies due west
   wings loving the air.

                                        Damp ground frozen hard
                                   the colt scrambles for footing
                Intent on browsing   cows and calves gather.
         elk don't notice my approach
             one scratches its ear.

From the far hilltop
the ranch appears a postcard
wonder who lives there?

On a rocky ridge
growing out of stone alone
the first pasque flower.

We race together
young hot colt between my thighs
no man can compare.

Twin redtails soar
as I stretch out in sagebrush
who is watching who?

Elk graze on new grass
scorched earth fans black from tree line
bitter work of man.

The colt trots six miles
legs like pistons—nostrils flared
sweet meadowlark notes.

White world pristine earth
snow has fallen all night long
nothing dares to move.

Scudding clouds—dark sky
we order his mom's headstone
gray granite gray sky.

Birds perch on bare sill
Flicker—Steller's jay—magpie
seeking feed in snow.

Frozen but still soft
orange-shafted flicker feathers
emerge from the snow.

Crooked wavy moon
thick depression-era glass
distorts his brave face.

Under the full moon
pewter light in snow melt pools
the coyotes call me.

So green the tansy
pushing from the deep snow drift
relishing the sun.

Heavy sheets falling
so strange to see rain on snow
which season is it?

White fragile blossom
growing out of sandy soil
Star of Bethlehem.

Sitting on a swing
the earth dips and sways beneath
my white-cracked bare feet.

The afternoon sun
pulls sticky sweat from pale skin
until clouds steal it.

Thick fog, low cold clouds
until sunlight breaks through mist
reveals open skies.

Frogs' chirping chorus
the new leaf-tatted aspens
how swiftly things change.

Green-headed Mallard
paddles upstream to his mate
she spins—swims away.

Half moon cloud-hidden
a coyote slinks through sagebrush
    antelope stands still.

            Twin sapsuckers fly
        screeching from power pole hole
            odd place for a home.

                    Frost-white spider web
                gleams in the hollow hoof trac[k]
                    who will soon fall prey?

Pincushion cactus
tiny spines—pale pink flowers
use care while sniffing.

Beside the still pond
purple loco—sand lilies
a blizzard rolls in.

Zebra-striped sphinx moth
flexes wet wings on a stone
 horse hooves just miss it.

                    Looking for summer
                the longing river runs fast
                     a robin flies past.

                                                        Sucking and slurping,
                                     the old horse drinks ditch water
                                           pussy willows bloom.

Houseflies in windows
bounce against sun-spotted glass
spider builds her web.

Curled brown on the vine
yellow banner wild sweet peas
victims of hard frost.

Bright as a set jewel
ruby-throated hummingbird
darts past surprised cat.

Canadian geese
waddle along river's edge
seeking a nest spot.

Black Mountain summit
slide rock—boulders—thick timber
far view of my world.

River voice bass deep
rolling water—silt and stones
I rest on the bridge.

Gray jay perched on pine
chirps and preens on highest branch
singing to the sky.

Full-curl big horn ram
timberline on Loveland Pass
rocks fall from his feet.

First wild iris blooms
light lavender and yellow
butterflies inspect.

The scent of horse sweat
the pull of hot flesh and bone
dandelions glow.

                                          Aspen leaves hang still
                                   this evening there is no breeze
                                            I untie my hair.

                Gilt-edged ring of light
          a trout rise—flashing leap—splash
                 did the fly escape?

White powder-puff butts
bounce above antelope legs
dust dances from hooves.

Honeysuckle vines
cloak the path with summer scent
deer wait in thick woods.

[to West Chester, Pennsylvania]

Lilac impressions
shift on sidewalk shade and sun
I jog on perfume.

Raven tries to fly
with plastic-wrapped candy stick
blood red in his beak.

Noontime sun bears down
every sweating pore open
the relief of breeze.

Bushy tail curling
gray squirrel clings to a park bench
waiting for handouts.

[home again]

Even in the house
I hear the bold frogs calling
mating season's short.

I find goose feathers
fluttering in meadow grass
coyote had a feast.

Snipe dive in night air
wind whistles through their bent wings
a poignant wooing.

Snowmelt slows—then stops
high peaks lose worn white clothing
river drops lower.

Silver locoweed
glistens in slow growing grass
makes cattle crazy.

Like white tissue tossed
the birdcage evening primrose
blooms in rocks and dust.

[Father's Day]

Walking through the sage
sunlight warming tall shadows
we stop—stare—then kiss.

Patterned black and white
dragonfly's gossamer wings
sparkle in sunlight.

Steel-blue cabbage moth
hugs a stone and stretches wings
preparing for flight.

Caught by the current
a willow branch bobs—dances
lightly with water.

Such testimony
tall penstemon and paintbrush
burnt orange greets purple.

Magpies squawk and fight
with an invading raven
what an alarm clock.

Intricate design
insect eggs on windowpane
strange incubation.

White stars in green glades
Richardson's geraniums
brighten underbrush.

Butterflies drift by
suspended on spider web
reflections of light.

What sweet smell draws me
to the overgrown creek bank
heart-leaf bittercress.

Shiny black beetle
crawling over red flagstones
where did you come from?

Mosquitoes annoy
worse than deer flies and horse flies
I swat swish stomp sigh.

Huge storm clouds gather
on the southern horizon
fast slash of lightning.

Five antelope snort
in brisk round-robin fashion
I am entertained.

Darkness into light
pregnant moon behind veiled clouds
metamorphoses.

Crowned head red-and-black
pileated woodpecker
clings to tall gatepost.

Hidden in dark sage
royal blue lupine candles
twin mourning doves call.

Pink fairy trumpets
tremble on slim fragile stems
shooting stars explode.

Waking from bad dreams
I ride along Copper Ridge
black bear stops to watch.

Between rhubarb plants
a profusion of daisies
glow white and bright gold.

Below the full moon
a nighthawk's wide white-barred wings
sing over sagebrush.

By the open grave
bouquets of bell-shaped flowers
grace dusty red ground.

[to Woodland Park]

All large eyes and ears
doe deer stands on the sidewalk
chewing sweet clover.

[to Vermont]

On a Vermont train
the flashing past of close trees
brilliant light shadow.

[in Sommerville, New Jersey]

Colony of wasps
builds a paper nest on screen
such activity.

[on Amtrak]

Under NYC
unusual air darkness
where is the sunshine?

[at Goddard College]

Endings beginnings
at dusk I walk the farm road
to *Silence's* grave.

Old hand-built stone arch
graces the upper garden
I stand there to pray.

Walking past midnight
the air is soft as shadow
telling me—lie down.

Screeching night heron
in the middle of my dreams
wakes me—shakes me still.

[home again]

Return to the ranch
cattle graze on hay meadows
here I find my heart.

Give me one more chance
to dance naked in moon light
capture childish joy.

Beneath the willows
an array of wild flowers
bloom in profusion.

Everything burns green
outside my bedroom window
   still I think of snow.

[12th Anniversary]

After many years
the heavy weight of marriage
   lifted by his kiss.

[to Gunnison]

Though a storm threatens
and the night wind changes fast
   no one wants a coat.

Sprig of lavender
sweet fragrance and fantasy
tangled in my hair.

Blood-plump raspberries
pulsed by sun—fattened with rain
warm clots in my hand.

Mourning dove's wings sing
through a silver rain-rinsed sky
I answer her cries.

A well-aged landscape
leans into the red sunset
day's blood sacrifice.

Clouds lined like limestone
horizon gray as granite
light rain humbles me.

I touch the night's nose
a fine chiseled ridge of bone
though the skin is soft.

                                        Across midnight's lips
                                  a wash of sheer want glimmers
                                        ahh don't wipe it off.

[home again]

I watch with wonder
white moths on delphiniums
rapid wash of wings.

Bear tracks on creek bank
show where a sow and her cub
paused for a dawn drink.

Thigh-high grass tassels
move in the breeze when I walk
I feel them tremble.

Black clouds beat back sun
stopped and stunned by the lightning
flashing in my eyes.

Finally dust settles
rain washes away pollen
from the dry sagebrush.

Every blade of grass
shivers with sparkling raindrops
each one a mirror.

Above the pine ridge
full moon sinks like a pink pearl
into the dawn sky.

Obscured by storm clouds
the hammered disk moon dangles
around day's white neck.

No rain is as pure
as that which falls steadily
after months of drought.

Just before sunset
trout break the lake's clear surface
slurping surface nymphs.

In early darkness
I find my way by foot feel
and the river's voice.

Gooseberries hang ripe
thorn-protected dark globules
sour juice and seeds.

Fragile fringed gentians
dot the verdant hay meadows
purple beauty marks.

Writing about rain
is necessary when it
falls incessantly.

Today the cat leaves
a chipmunk's thin furry tail
outside the front door.

Small magpie mummy
rests against the cat's food dish
the mouth still open.

Already flocking
robins cluster in aspens
singing gone south songs.

Red gray in sage green
a flash across the pasture
coyote races rain.

[to Woodland Park]

I hold mother's hand
a slow walk around the block
during mid-summer.

[at University of Colorado, Boulder]

King Lear's balmy night
crickets compete with actors
Shakespeare cannot win.

[return to Woodland Park]

I lie in the sun
squirrels pester me for peanuts
persistent beggars.

A hard rain wipes out
the long letter I wrote him
nature sets our course.

[my 47th birthday]

A blush flower gift
completely full and open
speaks words of sweetness.

                        Two huge pelicans
            wing beat the lake's smooth surface
                      sounding like thunder.

                                                          Explorer gentian
                                          perfect purple cupped chalice
                                              stemmed by oval leaves.

Horse snort—mid-day sun
grasshopper wings whir and click
my cares melt away.

Sweet to draw the bees
thick Canadian thistle
perfumes the night air.

One white daisy waves
from the wooden flower box
others killed by frost.

The lakes are quiet
pelicans and blue heron
patiently fishing.

Behind a cloud's veil
half moon hides a pretty face
I swear she's blushing.

Dark gray virga falls
in a perfectly blue sky
where do storms come from?

Eighteen antelope
desperately sprint sage flats
on ridge top bucks snort.

Horse fly on white shirt
I thought his life was over
where will he go now?

Between two cloud banks
a strip of buttermilk blue
foreshadows clear skies.

The only voice heard
is a cricket in a boat
sure to mean something.

Three days of fasting
I am as insubstantial
as a miller's wing.

The last pale asters
nod in a breath of fall breeze
saying yes to death.

Gold leaves fall like coins
making the wet forest floor
shine like caught treasure.

Night bull elk bugling
dawn cows squealing in timber
mating season songs.

Tiny spider webs
sparkle with frost and first light
sagebrush wears earrings.

A persistent gnat
buzzes around my right ear
I should have listened.

Autumn

From atop the ridge
the valley burns with color
rain is on the way.

Terrorist attack
in Hotevilla the Hopi knew
we eat mutton stew.

[headed for the Navajo Reservation]

Stopping at mountains
tobacco prayer offering
only vultures seen.

Leaving Window Rock
long miles of open desert
cleanse and purify.

[home again]

From the timbered ridge
a bull elk chortles and grunts
neck hairs stand erect.

Wet gooseberry-black
bear scat steams on the trail edge
I wait—hold my breath.

Walking in the dark
guided by the river's voice
I find my way home.

Sheltered from the frost
nodding in dense willow shade
a few last flowers.

Cathedral-like light
shines through yellow aspen leaves
silence shivers dawn.

Four coyotes circle
so close I see their pink tongues
as they pant and yip.

Sun and wind on skin
not one single thought intrudes
in this seduction.

A black beetle crawls
in sun over stones and sticks
stops in my shadow.

My face on rough bark
the old pine tree whispers low
hello granddaughter.

In the dark the sound
of moving grazing horses
brings me true comfort.

From thick underbrush
a cottontail rabbit runs
white tail a beacon.

Single aspen leaf
suspended on a sagebrush
glows like a cat's eye.

Dried beggar lice stick
to dog's ruff and shoelaces
oh to have that grip.

Brushed by the colt's legs
wild flag seedpods shiver-buzz
    like a rattlesnake.

        At noon the hot sun
        makes me forget about fall
        and coming winter.

                                                How the cows beller
                                  when their calves are hauled away
                                      new calves grow within.

Waking from a nap
on the banks of the river
white moths flutter by.

Chipped by other hands
little pieces of flint shine
in filtered sunlight.

Red-capped perfect sphere
rising behind far mountains
guide my husband home.

Cow path through thistles
prickly leaves and wet manure
no easy choices.

Vicious yips and howls
a coyote pack chews the night
around the full moon.

Dun colt in gold grass
wild flowers dried on the stem
paint this picture now.

Sitting in the sun
my back against a pine tree
I hear sap flowing.

Beetle-killed pinewood
round after round the stack grows
who will share my fire?

We walked many miles
across pastures and meadow
never said a word.

On this calm morning
nothing disturbs the lake's face
except the cold light.

Southern slant of sun
loves caressing naked skin
where I lie sleeping.

Black and white flutter
into a leafless aspen
magpie cleans his beak.

Pine branches crackle
in the pot-bellied wood stove
contentment in fire.

Sorting calves from cows
scrambling in manure and dust
autumn transition.

Spider in corner
web wrapped round a dozen flies
nifty housekeeper.

Wind out of the west
cuts like knife through coat to skin
will I make it home?

Three starlit ghost rocks
huddle like men under trees
what are they saying?

  A candle flame lights
the room's small interior
like the thought of love.

                    The forecast stays poor
                    the barometer falls fast
                      nothing stops winter.

                                                  Shedding their dry leaves,
                                                aspen trees blow in the wind
                                                  before the snow comes.

The last antelope
bolts across sagebrush pastures
kicking up the dust.

Racing up a post
chipmunk's horizontal tail
flags his get away.

Without calves, the cows
change from mothers to matrons
grow fat and content.

The landscape burns brown
even a skif of new snow
won't change fall's dry face.

                                        In hard driving wind.
                            I walk many miles backwards
                                  trying to catch up.

I thought rendezvous
meant a coming together
why are we silent?

Twin doves peck pebbles
until my approach sends them
flying to fence rails.

Cross-fox runs panting
along the graveled roadbed
dives for grass-lined ditch.

The fen's sphagnum moss
gives and bends—oozes water
trembles underfoot.

Waiting for daylight
I breathe within his circle
knowing death will come.

[to Buena Vista]

Two deer browse brush in
a Buena Vista front yard
a man cleans his car.

After my sauna
tumbling Cottonwood Creek
washes away sweat.

Moon caught in pine trees
silver light fights black branches
creating chaos.

Flies should not be here
buzzing offbeat summer songs
in frost-glazed windows.

Casting my shadow
sensual moon chases me
I long to be caught.

My old gelding stops
belly deep in the river,
drinks his fill then snorts.

Hard trot for long miles
one coyote—one antelope
the colt's coat shines sweat.

On these warm mornings
I walk the ranch boundaries
looking for my past.

No sound—no movement
the pine and aspen stand still
foreshadowing storm.

So terribly dry
blond grass crumbles to powder
cracked earth groans beneath.

First snow—second snow
third—doesn't really matter
landmarks disappear.

Chickadees peck seeds
next to slow retreating snow
black cat flicks his tail.

Timbered ridge at dawn
naked sky wearing black lace
sexy day waking.

Ducks flock to migrate
ice edges the riverbanks
changing water's song.

[To Austin for Texas Book Festival]

Texas air is warm
my heart begins to thaw out
and I burst open.

In a rum bottle
a Japanese fighting fish
swims in small circles.

Waiting is hard work
but I believe in morning's
easy healing cure.

I fear daily rain
will wash away well-made plans
in torrential floods.

How easily dreams
become stark reality
the night breathes through me.

When dawn comes again
the world has forever changed
because of water.

After a long nap
and soaking in the hot tub
I sweep fallen leaves.

[home again]

I walk by myself
is anything lonelier
than a big airport?

A thin skin of ice
shines aquamarine on lakes
waves are caught and held.

Ten chickadees flit
from ponderosa to spruce
searching for fresh seeds.

Bold coyote chorus
elk droppings on forest track
shadows grow longer.

Thanksgiving remnants
left as humble offering
coyote's great surprise.

I taste the dying
on a strong wind-flinging dust
the promise of snow.

High on my prayer ridge
west wind whips hair into eyes
I ask for courage.

Ten below zero
frozen river—frozen lakes
an unheard stillness.

Cows trail in for hay
leaving scuffed tracks in fresh snow
summer's forgotten.

In afternoon air
we trot miles into darkness
colt's steamy cloud breath.

Culvert caught water
gurgles free—the rest remains
ice-bound in moonlight.

A hole in gray clouds
allows one ray of sunlight
to shine on high peaks.

I will settle for
whatever winter brings me
as long as it's love.

White antelope butts
bright against dull sage brown grass
they circle around.

Pink streaked sunrise clouds
scuttle to the horizon
blown by unseen breeze.

Three does cross the road
regal bearing—flipping tails
trust the coming night.

Non-stop wind swirls dust
blows dirt straight east to Kansas
strange snowless winter.

Barely audible
snow buntings chirp and echo
the day's beginning.

Christmas tree spotted
snuggling a rusted wire fence
destined to be cut.

An owl's wings whisper
through the deep shadows of pine
snow weighted branches.

I ache for the way
the dry world sounds when it snows
haunted—holy—hushed.

Elk tracks milled around
the Trophy Lakes dusty shore
 in night's middle dark.

 I wonder if snow
 falls with any direction
  or if it just falls?

[husband's 70th birthday]

Another birthday
the years have run by so fast
 like an eye blinking.

Snow patterned landscape
horses graze white-gold patches
I watch from windows.

Meteor shower,
southwest sky before first light
I lose track of stars.

I spur to a lope
pushing the dun colt's limit
how big is his heart?

Nearly silent now
running on top of the ice
the river freezes.

The little hand saw
chews through a two-inch tree trunk
severing the pine.

Yes I decorate
as I do every Christmas
　　believing in joy.

　　　　　　The land does not know
　　　　　　that I celebrate its worth
　　　　　　　whenever I walk.

　　　　　　　　　　　　　　An aching inside
　　　　　　　　　　　tells me the year is coming
　　　　　　　　　　　　　quickly to a close.

Envision dying
on the shortest day of the year
envision living.

Searching for real joy
a presence out of thin air
what might I conjure?

Sorrel—buckskin—dun
the colors of my horses
paint the dull landscape.

Badger digs for voles
churning up dirt in big piles
constructing his world.

The cold seeps around
all manner of obstructions
except human hearts.

I wonder if snow
knows when we want it most
then decides "no show."

Thick shaggy horse hides
tell winter's temperatures
good thermometers.

Between dark layers
of receding wind-blown clouds
the curious moon.

Elk tracks and droppings
appear on the wooded trail
ghostly animals.

Ninety miles away
midnight fireworks on Pike's Peak
do animals watch?

Walking in starlight
brings back distant memories
boots quiet on dry earth.

Also by Laurie Wagner Buyer

Spring's Edge: A Ranch Wife's Chronicle, University of New Mexico Press

Selling Guns (audio cd), Del Sol Studios

Across the High Divide (poetry), Ghost Road Press

Side Canyons (fiction), Five Star/an imprint of Thomson-Gale

Red Colt Canyon (poetry), Music Mountain Press

Glass-eyed Paint in the Rain (poetry), High Plains Press

Little Dancing Fawn's Tale of Christmas Joy (childrens' story), Snowy Creek Press

Braintanning Buckskin: A Lesson for Beginners (poetry chapbook), Dry Crik Press

Blue Heron (poetry chapbook), Dry Crik Press

Information available at www.lauriewagnerbuyer.com

About the Poet

Photograph courtesy Wendy Jacobs

LAURIE WAGNER BUYER writes, speaks, performs, and teaches about women in the American West. She is the author of three collections of poetry, including *Across the High Divide*, winner of the WWA Spur Award. Her memoir, *Spring's Edge: A Ranch Wife's Chronicles*, was a 2009 finalist for the Colorado Book Award. *Infinite Possibilities* is her first collection of haiku and was written from her experiences as a ranch wife in Colorado's high country. Laurie now lives in Texas with her husband, songwriter and author W. C. Jameson.